There are two kinds of camels. Some have only one hump and are called dromedaries. They live in North Africa and Arabia.

Others have two humps and are called Bactrian camels. They live in central Asia.

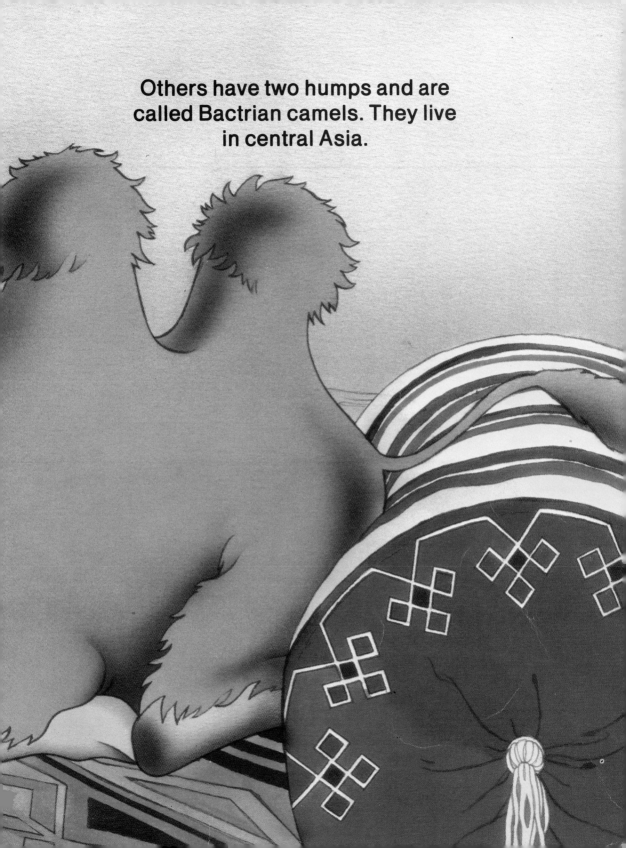

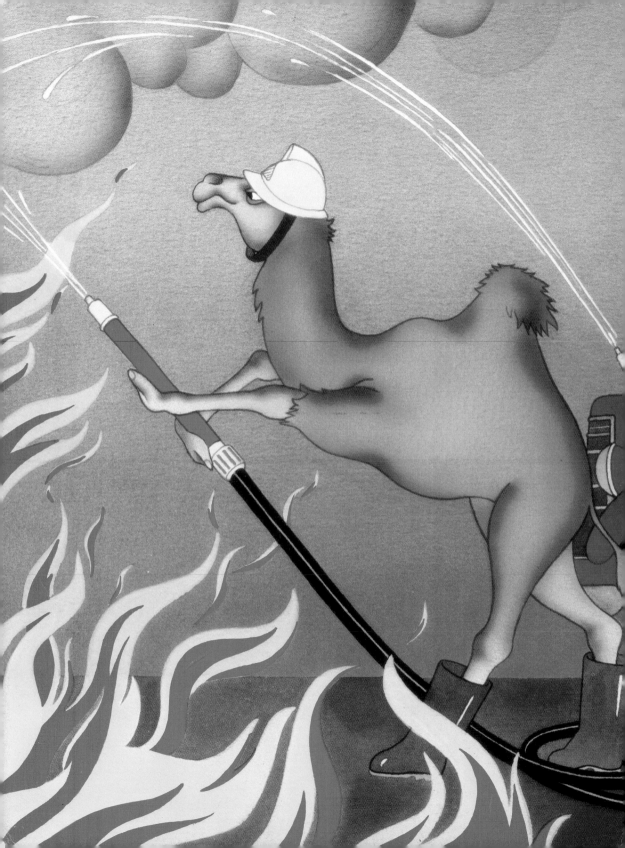

The camel lives in the desert
and can stand a lot of heat.

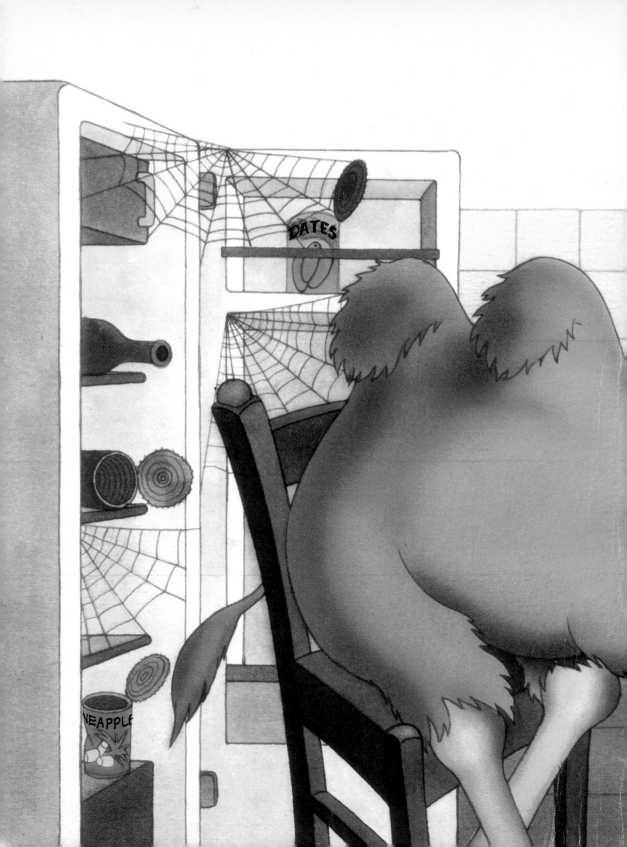

The camel can go many days
without eating or drinking.

A camel weighs about 1,500 pounds and can carry more than 500 pounds.

When a camel walks, its front
and back feet on each side
are in step.

Desert people use the
camel as transportation and
to carry things. The camel
also provides milk, meat,
wool and leather.

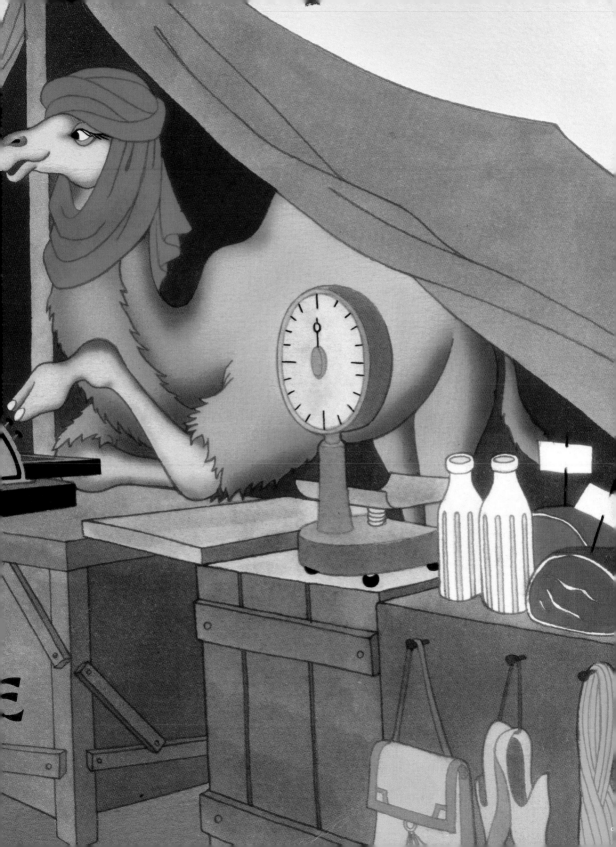

Camels are not very friendly. They hardly ever show interest in people.

Camels have been used instead of horses in desert wars.

Male camels get very irritated when their
mate is threatened. They will bite,
kick and even spit.

Mother camels have only one baby every two years. A few days after giving birth, the mother will go back to work carrying things with her baby trotting after her.